COMPOSER SHOWCASE
HAL LEONARD
STUDENT PIANO LIBRARY

Roller Coasters & Rides

EIGHT DUETS FOR ONE PIANO, FOUR HANDS

BY JENNIFER AND MIKE WATTS

T0070891

ISBN 978-1-4803-9805-4

HAL•LEONARD®
CORPORATION
7777 W. BLUEMOUND RD. P.O. BOX 13819 MILWAUKEE, WI 53213

In Australia Contact:
Hal Leonard Australia Pty. Ltd.
4 Lentara Court
Cheltenham, Victoria, 3192 Australia
Email: ausadmin@halleonard.com.au

Visit Hal Leonard Online at
www.halleonard.com

Performance Notes

Are We There Yet? (p. 4)

A lively piece in the style of old big band swing, students will hopefully feel the anticipation the title suggests! The secondo part is the big band rhythm section keeping the beat steady. The melodic phrases start in the primo part and are "answered" by phrases in the secondo part. Students can imagine the sound of a big band—with horn sections playing these different parts. Students might be encouraged to listen to Glen Miller's "I've Got a Gal in Kalamazoo" to get a feel for this type of music.

At the Top of the Ferris Wheel (p. 16)

A lyric waltz should be played gracefully with a feeling of "one." Measures 16–17 have a *ritardando* and an *a tempo* that will encourage careful listening to each other. Students will have a chance to thoughtfully add pedal at their own discretion. The primo part has phrases that sometimes start on the second beat of the measure. Students are encouraged to think about how to articulate the melody and keep the "waltz" feeling!

Don't Look Down! (p. 8)

Have you ever had to play the highest and lowest notes on the piano? This whimsical piece is dedicated to my students who have asked for this opportunity! Students become more familiar with octave denotations, as well as parallel movement. The primo section starts with four measures of 15ma, and then drops down a register in the middle of the composition. The last four measures are similar to the first four measures and use the highest treble note on the piano! In measures 10–11, the secondo part gets to play the lowest octave in the bass.

Jungle Grooveland (p. 12)

Warning! The urge to dance along to this piece is almost overwhelming!! It is in a "rhythm and blues" style. The goal is for both players to lock into the feel of this genre of "old Motown." The upbeats should be accented in order to get the right feel for this composition.

On the Carousel (p. 19)

Remember the ponies moving up and down? The primo has a melody in the RH with a LH accompaniment that is also melodic. Measures 24–25 will encourage careful listening between duet partners as the carousel slows and stops!

Roller Coaster's Revenge (p. 22)

Going on a roller coaster can be accompanied by mixed feelings! Students will recognize some peaceful parts of the ride by little melodies in D major, and then a diminished chord conveys the sharp turns and fear! Then the roller coaster is smooth again until the next sharp turn! Dynamics play a big part in achieving the "scary" feel of this piece!

The Water Slide (p. 28)

Climbing up and sliding down! Over and over, splashing into a pool of cool water! Dynamics are emphasized in this playful duet that should be felt in "one." Measure 15 begins a rhythmic interaction between players as well as a crescendo that helps set the tone for a big water slide descent!

Which Ride to Choose? (p. 25)

Students will enjoy the two moods presented in this duet. Classical phrases are paired with rock and roll responses! The Mozart-like classical sections are mezzo-piano and the "Rock out!" parts are forte, providing the dynamic contrast. Duet partners will enjoy the challenge of suddenly shifting genres. For an effective performance, students should communicate these different moods with enthusiasm!

This book is lovingly dedicated to my students. Thank you for allowing me to travel this music journey with you! I am continually inspired by you, and love to watch how understanding of music unfolds in all of you!

–Jennifer Watts

CONTENTS

Are We There Yet?

By Jennifer and Mike Watts

Don't Look Down!

(Have you ever had to play the highest and lowest notes?)

By Jennifer and Mike Watts

9

Jungle Grooveland

By Jennifer and Mike Watts

13

15

At the Top of the Ferris Wheel

By Jennifer and Mike Watts

On the Carousel

By Jennifer and Mike Watts

Roller Coaster's Revenge

By Jennifer and Mike Watts

Which Ride to Choose?

By Jennifer and Mike Watts

27

The Water Slide

By Jennifer and Mike Watts

The Big Climb Up!

COMPOSER SHOWCASE
HAL LEONARD STUDENT PIANO LIBRARY

This series showcases great original piano music from our **Hal Leonard Student Piano Library** family of composers, including Bill Boyd, Phillip Keveren, Carol Klose, Jennifer Linn, Mona Rejino, Eugénie Rocherolle and more. Carefully graded for easy selection, each book contains gems that are certain to become classics!

BILL BOYD

JAZZ BITS (AND PIECES)
Early Intermediate Level
00290312 11 Solos............................$7.99

JAZZ DELIGHTS
Intermediate Level
00240435 11 Solos............................$7.99

JAZZ FEST
Intermediate Level
00240436 10 Solos............................$7.99

JAZZ PRELIMS
Early Elementary Level
00290032 12 Solos............................$6.99

JAZZ SKETCHES
Intermediate Level
00220001 8 Solos............................$7.99

JAZZ STARTERS
Elementary Level
00290425 10 Solos............................$6.99

JAZZ STARTERS II
Late Elementary Level
00290434 11 Solos............................$7.99

JAZZ STARTERS III
Late Elementary Level
00290465 12 Solos............................$7.99

THINK JAZZ!
Early Intermediate Level
00290417 Method Book............................$10.99

DEBORAH BRADY

PUPPY DOG TALES
Elementary Level
00296718 5 Solos............................$6.95

TONY CARAMIA

JAZZ MOODS
Intermediate Level
00296728 8 Solos............................$6.95

SUITE DREAMS
Intermediate Level
00296775 4 Solos............................$6.99

SONDRA CLARK

DAKOTA DAYS
Intermediate Level
00296521 5 Solos............................$6.95

FAVORITE CAROLS FOR TWO
Intermediate Level
00296530 5 Duets............................$7.99

FLORIDA FANTASY SUITE
Intermediate Level
00296766 3 Duets............................$7.95

ISLAND DELIGHTS
Intermediate Level
00296666 4 Solos............................$6.95

THREE ODD METERS
Intermediate Level
00296472 3 Duets............................$6.95

For full descriptions and song lists for the books listed here, and to view a complete list of titles in this series, please visit our website at www.halleonard.com

MATTHEW EDWARDS

CONCERTO FOR YOUNG PIANISTS
FOR 2 PIANOS, FOUR HANDS
Intermediate Level Book/CD
00296356 3 Movements $16.95

CONCERTO NO. 2 IN G MAJOR
FOR 2 PIANOS, 4 HANDS
Intermediate Level Book/CD
00296670 3 Movements............................$16.95

PHILLIP KEVEREN

MOUSE ON A MIRROR
Late Elementary Level
00296361 5 Solos............................$6.95

MUSICAL MOODS
Elementary/Late Elementary Level
00296714 7 Solos............................$5.95

ROMP!
A DIGITAL KEYBOARD ENSEMBLE FOR SIX PLAYERS
Intermediate Level
00296549 Book/CD............................$9.95

SHIFTY-EYED BLUES
Late Elementary Level
00296374 5 Solos............................$6.99

TEX-MEX REX
Late Elementary Level
00296353 6 Solos............................$6.99

CAROL KLOSE

CORAL REEF SUITE
Late Elementary Level
00296354 7 Solos............................$6.99

DESERT SUITE
Intermediate Level
00296667 6 Solos............................$7.99

FANCIFUL WALTZES
Early Intermediate Level
00296473 5 Solos............................$7.95

GARDEN TREASURES
Late Intermediate Level
00296787 5 Solos............................$7.99

ROMANTIC EXPRESSIONS
Intermediate/Late Intermediate Level
00296923 5 Solos............................$8.99

WATERCOLOR MINIATURES
Early Intermediate Level
00296848 7 Solos............................$7.99

JENNIFER LINN

AMERICAN IMPRESSIONS
Intermediate Level
00296471 6 Solos............................$7.99

CHRISTMAS IMPRESSIONS
Intermediate Level
00296706 8 Solos............................$6.99

JUST PINK
Elementary Level
00296722 9 Solos............................$6.99

LES PETITES IMAGES
Late Elementary Level
00296664 7 Solos............................$7.99

LES PETITES IMPRESSIONS
Intermediate Level
00296355 6 Solos............................$7.99

REFLECTIONS
Late Intermediate Level
00296843 5 Solos............................$7.99

TALES OF MYSTERY
Intermediate Level
00296769 6 Solos............................$7.99

MONA REJINO

CIRCUS SUITE
Late Elementary Level
00296665 5 Solos............................$5.95

JUST FOR KIDS
Elementary Level
00296840 8 Solos............................$7.99

MERRY CHRISTMAS MEDLEYS
Intermediate Level
00296799 5 Solos............................$7.99

PORTRAITS IN STYLE
Early Intermediate Level
00296507 6 Solos............................$7.99

EUGÉNIE ROCHEROLLE

ENCANTOS ESPAÑOLES (SPANISH DELIGHTS)
Intermediate Level
00125451 6 Solos............................$7.99

JAMBALAYA
FOR 2 PIANOS, 8 HANDS
Intermediate Level
00296654 Piano Ensemble............................$9.99

JAMBALAYA
FOR 2 PIANOS, 4 HANDS
Intermediate Level
00296725 Piano Duo (2 Pianos)............................$7.95

TOUR FOR TWO
Late Elementary Level
00296832 6 Duets............................$7.99

TREASURES
Late Elementary/Early Intermediate Level
00296924 7 Solos............................$8.99

CHRISTOS TSITSAROS

DANCES FROM AROUND THE WORLD
Early Intermediate Level
00296688 7 Solos............................$6.95

LYRIC BALLADS
Intermediate/Late Intermediate Level
00102404 6 Solos............................$8.99

POETIC MOMENTS
Intermediate Level
00296403 8 Solos............................$8.99

SONATINA HUMORESQUE
Late Intermediate Level
00296772 3 Movements............................$6.99

SONGS WITHOUT WORDS
Intermediate Level
00296506 9 Solos............................$7.95

THROUGHOUT THE YEAR
Late Elementary Level
00296723 12 Duets............................$6.95

ADDITIONAL COLLECTIONS

ALASKA SKETCHES
by Lynda Lybeck-Robinson
Early Intermediate Level
00119637 8 Solos............................$7.99

AMERICAN PORTRAITS
by Wendy Stevens
Intermediate Level
00296817 6 Solos............................$7.99

AT THE LAKE
by Elvina Pearce
Elementary/Late Elementary Level
00131642 10 Solos and Duets............................$7.99

COUNTY RAGTIME FESTIVAL
by Fred Kern
Intermediate Level
00296882 7 Rags............................$7.99

PLAY THE BLUES!
by Luann Carman (Method Book)
Early Intermediate Level
00296357 10 Solos............................$9.99

HAL•LEONARD®
CORPORATION
7777 W. BLUEMOUND RD. P.O. BOX 13819 MILWAUKEE, WI 53213